The Prayer of Surrender
By Master El Morya

Beloved Father/Mother God, into Thy hands I commend my being. Use my love, my thoughts, and my life in selfless service to Thee. Release from me all that hinders the fulfillment of my holy purpose and Ascension. Teach me to be kind in the ways of the Brotherhood of Light. Direct and establish my lifestream in ways that, daily and hourly, my true identity in God becomes my reality.

Beloved God Presence I AM,
Eternal Father/Mother God,
May the covenant I made with Thee
Be totally fulfilled!
May I live my life to feel
Your Love and see Your Light!
May Your Will manifest on Earth
As it is in Heaven!
Into Thy hands I surrender my being,
That through me, God be glorified in all things!
So be it, Beloved I AM.

CUBA:

Resurrecting the Amethyst Isle

A Book of Prophecies

Rev. Rina A. González

C U B A:
Resurrecting the Amethyst Isle
A Book of Prophecies

Self-Published in the USA
By Rina A. González
Published © 2011

ISBN # 978-0-9792408-3-6

PROPHECIES THAT HEAL EARTH,

MIND, HEART & SOUL

As send by
The Ascended Dear Ones

Saint Germain
El Morya
Sananda
Kuthumi
Mother Mary
Archangel Raphael
Archangel Michel
Archangel Jophiel
Archangel Zadkiel
Holy Amethyst
to

Reverend Rina A. González

Thanks and appreciation to these wonderful Co-Servers of the Light for their inspirational work:

Elizabeth Clare Prophet, Co-Founder of "The Summit Light House" http://tsl.org/
Lori Adaile Toye, Founder of "I AM AMERICA"
http://www.iamamerica.com/
Aurelia Louise Jones, Founder and Owner of Mt. Shasta Light Publishing and the Lumurian Connection Network:
http://mslpublishing.com
Oceanógrafa, Paulina Zelitsky http://s8int.com/water27.html

INDEX

Introduction	9
About Rev. Rina	11
Underwater City Found	14
One of the many theories about Atlantis	16
The Mysticism, Esoteric, and Spiritual powers of …	23
Kali Yuga and the Birth of a Golden Age	28
Affirmations & Decrees [several]	31
Preparing Body, Mind & Soul for Ascension	55
What is Ascension?	57
Preparing the Astral Body Ready for Ascension	59
Etheric Temple ~ Retreat	64
Revealing the Secrets Powers of …	67
Awakening the Eight-Sided Cell of Perfection	69
The importance of a Vegetarian Diet	75
Grace	80
Preparing the Evolutionary Body	81
Connecting the human E. B. to Earths'	84
Humanity's Struggles	87
Cuba's Golden City, Vortex and Stars	91
Call to the Illumination Flame	97
Under The Cuban Sky ~ Information	98
Seminar, Workshops and Classes	99
I Am Divine [Poem]	100

DEDICATION

This book is in appreciation to the courageous and sensitive individuals who have made this lifetime more than a mere existence, for in so doing they have given life meaning, completion, and wholeness.

I thank you for being a free thinker, for having an adventurous sprit and for not allowing meritocracy to stand in the way of progress or reasoning.

I know that I AM in the presence of greatness when I see one of my brothers or sisters being who they truly are at whatever cost, or when I see one of them stand behind their convictions.

I know that I am in the presence of greatness when one of you takes the time to give freely from your hearts; this action reflects the purity of your intensions, and shows the strength of your soul.

To all luminous sons and daughters of the stars who have walked the earth for eons, and who have tirelessly worked to better life on Planet Earth. Thank you for sharing your light, vision, and wisdom with others. To all light workers who share their love, compassion, and devotion, in the name of Love, I salute thee!

In Peace, Love, and Light,

I AM, Rev. Rina A. González

INTRODUCTION

This book of prophecies gives the reader the choice of reaching enlightenment in this incarnation, if this is what the individual desires.

In it, the seeker will find metaphysical teachings, decrees, and affirmations meant to shift the density of the body from our Third Dimension, to a lighter version of self, thus initiating the process of moving onto the Fourth, Fifth Dimension and beyond.

One of the reasons why at this time humanity feels a disconcerting unrest is because Our Dear Planet is in transition. We, as her children are answering the call as more and more of us are seeking to learn, and as we do, our minds, hearts, and souls grow and expand. In so doing, are guaranteed reaching not only our full mastery in this lifetime, even more importantly, with full recognition of our spiritual powers, we will reach **"Unana", The Consciousness of Oneness.**

In this book, key topics on how to prepare for the upcoming Earth Changes will be addressed. Such as, how by making the Astral Body [luminous body], and the Evolutionary Body [the 6th outer aura] ready for Ascension along side Mother Earth, could safe our life.

I do intent on giving information on the importance of changing our diet to a well balanced vegetarian one, and how to keep our bodies, [temples] clean and energized at all times and why.

I will reveal Cuba's mysticism, esoteric and spiritual powers, and the role that Cuba and her spiritual powers have played on Planet Earth for millions of years.

We will also teach the protocol to be followed when visiting Golden Cities, their Vortices, and Stars, located strategically throughout the Planet. I want to express the importance of respecting these sites, for while those traveling to them might not know this, they indeed are stepping onto Hollowed Grounds. All who go should be mindful when stepping on to these holy sites and while there, upkeep the energies of this holy place intact for those that follow by showing reverence.

In Peace, Light and Love,

I AM Rev. Rina

ABOUT REV. RINA

Rina A. González was born in Havana, Cuba in the mid 40's. She worked in accounting for 35 years for various well-known companies raising her three children as a single mother. Since early in life, she felt the need to search for life's deeper meaning, which she calls 'truth'. During her many years of searching for 'life's truth'', Rina was lead to find Metaphysics and immediately felt that she had come home. She liked the subject so much that studying it became her life's mission. In so doing, she realized that the more she probed into the 'life's truth' the more that the true nature of life was revealed. In time, she discovered her 'truth' and it was so powerful that she could no longer deny its existence or that she had to comply with her soul's desire.

From then on, Rina devoted her life to the service of humanity, where she employed her spiritual gifts or abilities to help those that came to her. Among these gifts or abilities is the fact that Rina was born a Spiritual Healer, a Physic, a Clairvoyant, and a Mystic. In time and under the sponsorship of the Brotherhood of Light and Ascended Master Saint Germain, Rina was ordained a Minister of Divinity, May 19, 1996.

Rina is a published author and her work reflects her commitment to bettering life on Planet Earth. To Rina, life is simple and too quickly complicated by a confused state of mind. As an observer of life, Rina writes about humanity's struggles, knowing that any negative behavior can only serve to deplete our energies, which in turn makes matters worse.

She has worked tirelessly for the 'Awakening of The Goddess Within'. Rina knows how precious every woman is and how important a roll each one plays in bringing Peace and Love to our lives, homes, loved ones, society, work place and to our Beloved Planet Terra. To Rina, ushering in 'The New Age of Enlightenment' is of great importance and a task that she does not take lightly. It is in recognizing the need in humanity to find peace in the midst of chaos and the importance of the times, why Rina does not slow her pace and continuously creates workshops, classes, and publishes books, in the hopes of creating the impetus that will give faith to the masses in our hour of need.

Passion moves her. And the energy of her passion goes into everything she does knowing that what she gives is the Harmonizing Energy of Love. Rina's love for humanity is real. She keeps the spark of hope alive so that the day will come when humanity can free itself from the constant struggle brought about by their collective [ignorance, greed, selfishness, =] confusion.

In the near future, Rina will be conducting classes on behalf of the , 'I AM AMERICA' movement sponsored by the Brotherhood of Light, and Ascended Master Saint Germain, were the upcoming prophecies for the world will be addressed. Rina and other instructors from this wonderful organization will guide the students to a better understanding of the events as well as discussing the 'Golden Cities, their Vortices', Stars, in their various locations.

Her recent trip to Cuba, after 48 years of absence, gave her an inside look into what she would be doing next. The love she felt and saw while in Cuba, moved her so much that upon her return she created **'Under the Cuban Sky'**, a site for the upcoming Spiritual Journeys to her blessed homeland.

While there, Rina had a sense of having come home, not only to the land of her birth, but she also become aware of the deep 'spiritual truth' that her island embodies. What is even more amazing is that although Cuba has been in a tug of war with countries and governments of opposing views, the land, and her people have remained blessed because of her immeasurable mystical, esoteric, and spiritual powers.

After all the years of longing, Rina had finally come home to find that what she felt and knew to be true was alive and thriving. The love, compassion, and laughter of the Cuban People are a welcoming sight. For Rina, it was more than coming home. It was her inescapable truth staring her right in the face, making her laugh and cry at the same time.

Today, Rina shares Cuba's Spiritual Wisdom and Love with the world in her book *'CUBA: Resurrecting the Amethyst Isle'* knowing that the information in it is vital and deeply connected to the upcoming World Changes. And as Cuba stands ready to serves the world, as a conduit of light, love, and compassion, so does Rev. Rina.

UNDERWATER CITY FOUND OFF CUBA'S COAST

Why is humanity fascinated by what happened millions of years ago if not because somewhere inside of us, we know that indeed these events did take place and what is more interesting, is that many of us were part of the experience. All esoteric knowledge is encoded in our memory cells. Anytime we hear talks about the Lost Continent of Atlantis, instinctively we know that the continent is not lost; it is resting, waiting for its resurrection.

Ever since I can remember, I have known that the Continent of Atlantis existed, even knew where it was located. The picture of its located is sketched in my mind. To me, it is real, vivid; so much, that I have no problem accepting this picture resembling what I had envisioned years ago.

Knowing how spirit works, I am sure that there are more than two of us with the same thought on Planet Earth presently. Even find it comical that as one drew a picture of its location, another created a web site, as I was inspired to write this book. As if the children of Atlantis, alive today, living in different parts of the world, had received subluminal message from Atlantis, letting us know that the time for her resurrection is near.

I marvel at creation and her work. I love all that is sublime and magical in life, for it never stops giving. Is a matter of fact the more time I dedicate to finding a deeper meaning to life, the more that life reveals its finest treasures, as was the case of *Paulina Zelitsky.*

Paulina Zelitsky said. ~ `It is stunning. What we see in our high-resolution sonar images are limitless rolling, white sand plains and, in the middle of this beautiful white sand, there are clear manmade large size architectural designs. It looks like when you fly over an urban development on a plane and you can see highways, tunnels and buildings."

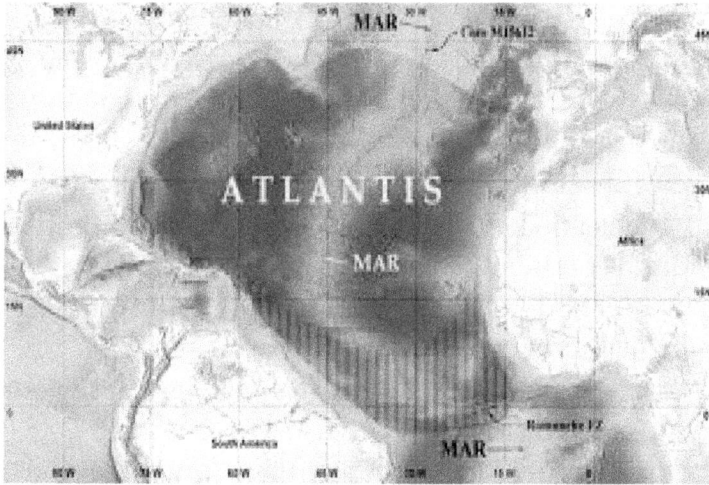

Magic lives in the heart that holds the possibility that life begins in the wink of an eye, in the flight of a butterfly, in a grain of sand, as much as in an atom. Therefore, for the glory of all that is just, true and noble in our hearts, minds and souls, let the magic begin by discovering the many possibilities allotted us!

ONE OF THE MANY THEORIES ABOUT ATLANTIS
By Paulina Zelitsky

Impossible, how huge and geometrically precise stone constructions, could had withstood the ravage of time, if not by the will of the gods. Unlike the theories about the Bermuda Triangle and Atlantis, the pyramids are decidedly real. What comes under scrutiny, are their origin, their possible mystical properties, and whether any Atlantis relics have been found on the ocean floor.

It has been longed argued that the ancient Egyptians and Aztecs could not possibly have built the pyramids on their own; therefore, the evidence of some greater intelligence, possibly extraterrestrial helped them to achieve these undertakings. But the earthly tools used in their construction have been found, and, while the pyramids represent an astonishing feat of engineering that required untold years of labor, it appears that early humans were capable of the task.

Some have focused on the amazing structural and geometrical properties of the pyramids. First, there is their incredible longevity: the pyramids have remained intact while other structures of a comparable age have crumbled away. This is largely attributable to the inherent durability of their characteristic shape. "It is, in fact, the form that a structure takes when it falls down!" James Randi has observed." In other words, having tumbled to a pyramid-shaped mass, it cannot collapse much further. "Therefore, their well-preserved state owes more to their architects' wisdom than to any mystical force.

Pyramid enthusiasts have derived remarkable mathematical formulas from the monuments' heights, lengths, and angles. This is especially true of the Great Pyramid of Cheops. Writers such as Erich von Daniken and Charles Piazzi Smyth have wrung all manner of figures out of this pyramid's measurements, including the Earth's polar radius and its distance in miles from the sun -- but their calculations take liberties that keep them from holding up under scrutiny. Furthermore, one can play with any set of figures and eventually produce false results that were never intended to be there. Martin Gardner demonstrated this by calculating the speed of light from the height and capstone weight of the Washington Monument.

Then again, maybe some geometrical phenomena were built into the pyramids -- if inadvertently. For instance, if you double the length of one base side of the Great Pyramid and divide it by the height, the result is very close to the value of **pi.** There is no evidence that the ancient Egyptians ever measured **pi.** One explanation is that the builders used a wheel tool to measure lengths, and using a circle's diameter as a unit of measure could lead to **pi.,** being "hidden" throughout the structure.

Pyramids have historically been viewed as repositories or conduits of otherworldly power. Egyptians used them to honor the dead and Aztecs performed ceremonial sacrifices on top of them, suggesting that the structures held a great deal of spiritual significance in both cultures.

These supposed spiritual properties, were brought to the attention of the modern world, by Karl Drbal, a Czechoslovakian, who in 1959 founded the notion of "Pyramid Power." It became fashionable to use miniature pyramids for the supposed purposes of magical healing, augmented psychic powers, and communion with alien beings. People believed that a wish written on a paper and worn inside a pyramid pendant would come true, and that an old razor blade placed in a pyramid would spontaneously become sharpen overnight.

Edgar Cayce, the prophet and Atlantis supporter, determined with his psychic powers, that the Great Pyramid was built by a team of Egyptians and Atlanteans. He said the Atlanteans helped by levitating the stones during construction, and that they recorded the whole of human history -- past and future -- within the pyramid. This comprehensive documentation ran up through 1998, in Cayce's projected 'Second Coming of Christ'.

If the folks from Atlantis were interested in pyramids, it stands to reason that they would have built some for themselves. There have been sightings of undersea objects that looked like pyramids from above the surface, which turned out to be natural formations with no pyramid shape at all. An elaborate Atlantis pyramid hoax was perpetrated in Charles Berlitz's 1978 in a book he titled, *Without a Trace,* the follow-up to his notorious, *The Bermuda Triangle.*

Berlitz presented sonar tracings of the Atlantic Ocean Floor near the island of Bimini as evidence of a giant sunken pyramid. Bimini lies within the Bermuda Triangle, and is in the exact area where Edgar Cayce placed Atlantis. Berlitz indicated that the pyramid reached 470 feet above the ocean floor and was 520 feet long at each of its four bases -- comparable in size to the 450-foot-high of the Great Pyramid.

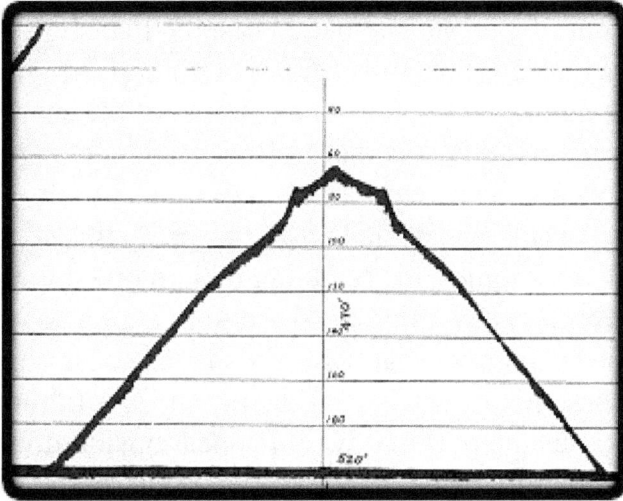

The sonar chart obtained by Captain Don Henry, purportedly showing a gigantic underwater "pyramid."

The sonar chart, obtained by Captain Don Henry and "authenticated" by Dr. J. Manson Valentine of the Miami Museum of Science, does indeed appear to constitute impressive proof... at least, until you know how to read it properly. The tracing shows a cross-section of a distinct, symmetrical pyramid shape rising above an otherwise flat surface. However, sonar tracing of the type Henry used produces a readout with a greatly exaggerated vertical axis, to make it easier to detect horizontal surface changes. Thus, what appears to be pyramid sides sharply rising at 45° angles is in reality a gentle slope of no more than two or three degrees. The furthest thing from 470 feet, the apex of this "pyramid" is really only a few feet tall.

To add to the deception, Berlitz pointed out the bottom line of the chart as representing the ocean floor. It was actually just an arbitrary line where the chart cut off; on such sonar charts, the line showing the true ocean floor runs off the bottom of the chart and reappears at the top. The contrast of the sharp slope against this false ocean floor made the map's subjects much more pyramid-like.

It is also possible that Henry made this sonar tracing by running his scanning boat in one direction, then abruptly reversing his direction. Doing so would produce a symmetrical pyramid-shaped sonar chart from practically any part of the ocean floor (although sometimes the pyramid would appear upside-down, depending on the slope and the boat's direction).

Berlitz also reported another alleged Atlantis ruin, in the "Bimini Road.", where he alleges that an undersea ribbon of parallel rock formations running for 1,000 miles off the Bimini coast were the remnants of a highway paved by Atlanteans. While the Bimini Road patterns do make it look like man-made, it is actually just an aggregation of beach rock, which naturally forms like this in many parts of the world.

One cannot say, whether Berlitz genuinely believed that the pyramids were there and that the Bimini Roads were indeed real, or if he had intentionally twisting the facts for the sake of another exciting bestseller. Although one wonders if as experts in their fields, Captain Henry and Dr. Valentine failed to point out to Berlitz his wild misconceptions.

The three legends, the Bermuda Triangle, Atlantis and the pyramids are remarkably complimentary to one another. Pyramids were built in both Africa and the Americas, and Atlantis served as a possible bridge to bring the concept to both places, as well as been needed for their architectural skills to both sides of the ocean. Atlantis's technological wreckage gives cause to strange occurrences in the Bermuda Triangle. All three stories deal with mysterious energies, ancient secrets, spirituality and death -- and possibly aliens, who might well be responsible for the whole shebang.

In science, when the findings of disparate fields of study dovetail into a harmonious whole, the result can be a mutual affirmation of validity. It may be tempting to follow the same line of thinking in the case of these three phenomena: "It all fits together so well, there *must* be something to it!" However, when the pieces include myths, half-truths and deception, the completed picture will be just a bunch of lies... or, at best, some really cool mythology.

Source: Paulina Zelitsky http://s8int.com/water27.html

THE MYSTICISM, ESOTERIC AND SPIRITUAL POWERS OF CUBA

It is my honor to give the world the mysticism, esoteric and spiritual powers of my native country, the beautiful Island of Cuba.

Everyone who has ever visited this lovely island leaves her with the feeling of longing and belonging without knowing why. Everyone feels a pull towards the country and towards its' people not understanding why. Those who speak Spanish find the conversation amicable and those who do not will always find a Cuban who speak theirs.

The vacationers find that they can do anything in this island paradise. Those who like the nightlife will find it easily. Those who want to go to beaches have the best to choose from. Those who want to learn more about Cuba's History or Culture will find museums all over the cities, or a Cuban at a corner ready to tell stories about his homeland. However, no journey to Cuba would be complete without learning about her mysticism, esoteric influence, and spiritual origin.

It is amazing how those who travel to Cuba feel as if time had stood still when there as well as noticing that their digestion improves in only days. A sense of euphoria comes over the visitors as the tropical breeze touches their skin and the musical notes of this tropical paradise enters the mind, heart, and soul, beating in unison, awakening all their senses.

When the visitors leave, feel that a part of them has stayed behind. Amazed at the experience, upon their return, tell their friends, and loved ones, to find that few understand what they are talking about. I understand how anyone traveling to Cuba feels a pull towards her. I who was born there, and who have lived many years in the States, upon my return in mid 2011, felt her pull charismatic pull immediately. Those that have never gone to Cuba do not understand how a country who has been subjected to 47 years of embargo could have anything to offer. Or how can a country under a dictatorship since 1959 have any beauty or grace left to give? My dear ones, the answer lies in her mysticism, esotericism, and spiritual powers.

We could say that Cuba's essence is like honey. While we can talk about how sweet honey is, how nourishing and good for the health, until the person tries it, they will never know what they are missing.

You see what few know is that many years ago, millions to be exact, Cuba was known, as the *Amethyst Isle*. Her land mass was greater then and as today, served as the connecting points or ports to other neighboring lands. Presently Cuba's Code of Arms, has key, on top in the middle. The word Cuba means Key and to this day, geographically, Cuba is the connector, they key, the pathway to other lands.

The Amethyst Stone is beautiful, strong, and has healing powers as well as can influence monetary gain. In the spiritual realm, an Amethyst is revered because of its transmuting energy. It is the strongest and most purifying energy known, in our three dimensional world, in the ether, and throughout the entire Universe.

Years later, Cuba became part of Atlantis as a focal point to the entire world. People found its Violate Flame and Light coming from the Temple of Purification where all pending karma was transmuted and purified. Then, the temple was seen physically from other neighboring countries.

Presently the Temple of Purification is in the ether over the Island of Cuba. It is located in the center of the island, in the Province of Villa Clara, in the town of Sancti Spiritus, in the beautiful beach of Ancon.

Stories have surfaced in regards to people experiencing healings in this area without knowing what to attribute their healing to. Throughout time, there have been reports of a light shining over the coastal water at night. Those who have ventured into the light have met its gravitational pull, never to come out again. Cuba's Archipelago is close in proximately to the Bermuda Triangle, evidence that the temple that ones stood there in the physical has remained in place in the ether. To a lesser degree, some of this temple's healing energies are found in some of South Florida beaches.

If this was not enough, this lovely island has a Golden City Vortex and its Star located in the City of Santa Clara; more information, later in the book.

During the upcoming World Changes, Cuba again will serve as a connecting point between neighboring lands. As Atlantis rises out of the deep blue waters off Cuba's Coast, her shape will change as well as other Central and South American Countries. Yet Cuba's center will remain intact, protecting its

Golden City, Vortex, Star, and Etheric Temple.

Cuba will be dressed in new garments, ready to serve the world and humanity, as she has always done. Cuba, as well as other countries will usher in The New World Order as "The Awakening of the Christ Consciousness enters Planet Earth".

Cuban scientists are reporting that by the year 2,050 many parts of Cuba will be under water. There are reports stating that Oriente, the most eastern point of Cuba, has already lost land mass. Other reports state that this is also true for beaches in other Cuban Provinces.

While part of whom I am feels compassion for all who will undergo these changes, knowing the significance and importance of the upcoming events all things considered, I am moved to see that my country has chosen to serve yet again as a conduit of light, love, and freedom for mankind.

Cuba has other well-kept secret. One of which is the true meaning behind the loved felt in this lovely island. While her humanity and warmth can be felt, few know what to attribute this to.

Among Cuba's emblems, there is one that holds the secret to her loving energy, this particular emblem is in the Cuban Flag, in her Code of Arms, and is the crown jewel of our Patron Saint, "La Virgen de la Caridad del Cobre". This emblem is a Star. Cuban's call her, "La Estrella Solitaria". However, throughout the Universe, this star is known as Venus, The Morning Star ~ The Goddess of Love.

Question: When are you going to Cuba? I cannot wait to get back. Except next time I go, I am going to thank her for her selfless service to humanity and to the world. I will see her under her true light; the light of love, grace, peace, and compassion that she so proudly embodies.

With all my love, *I am a proud daughter of my beloved homeland, Cuba La Bella!*

KALI YUGA AND THE BIRTH
OF A GOLDEN AGE
by Lori Adaile Toye

Man has spent ages developing systems that map the cycles of change. Many of these ancient systems measure the movement of forces based upon equinoxes and solstices. Astrology uses the movement of constellations, to calculate the influence of energy in motion, on all created things. Since all things change and move, the Ancients knew that understanding this movement would help them to understand the tendencies of the future. It's always nice to know if you're going up and it's always nice to prepare for your landing when you're going down.

The Greek mystics taught that the world would always travel through four ages: the Golden Age, the Silver Age, the Bronze Age, and the Iron Age. This teaching closely resembles the four Yugas of the Hindus: Krita - Yuga, Treta - Yuga, Dvapara - Yuga, and Kali –Yuga.

Their calculation is based upon the twelve signs of the zodiac and is as follows: "In each of the 12 signs [the zodiac], there are 1,800 minutes; multiply this number by 12 you get 21,600; e.g. 1,800 x 12 = 21,600.

Multiply this 21,600 by 80 and it will give 1,728,000, which is the duration of the first age, called Krita -Yuga. If the same number be multiplied by 60, it will give 1,296.000, the years of the second age, Treta – Yuga. The same number multiplied by 40 gives 864,000, the length of the third age, Dvapara –

Yuga. The same multiplied by 20 gives 432,000, the fourth age, Kali – Yuga." Each of these four ages represent the cycles of duration of all things, birth, growth, maturity and decay.

The Ancients and Sages who structured these incredible systems are gone, but the Ages and the Yugas march on, charting the patterns of motion that can still tell us a lot about today and tomorrow.

According to sources, we are still living out the age of Iron, the cycle of decay, Kali-Yuga. But, there's good news. After this cycle is complete, the teeter-totter raises back up and we enter into a cycle of birth that will last over 1.5 millions of years, The Golden Age, Krita-Yuga.

I have merged these ancient teachings with Ascended Master Teachings in the chart that follows. Here, you will see that the age that we are currently experiencing, is paving the pathway for the age of Gold. *{Kali-Yuga is the Iron Age, age of industrialization ruled by money, symbolized by the suit of coins in the Tarot. According to sources, this age began in the year 3,102 B.C. Six thousand years before the end of Dvapara – Yuga, when the continent of Atlantis sunk into the now Atlantic Ocean}.*

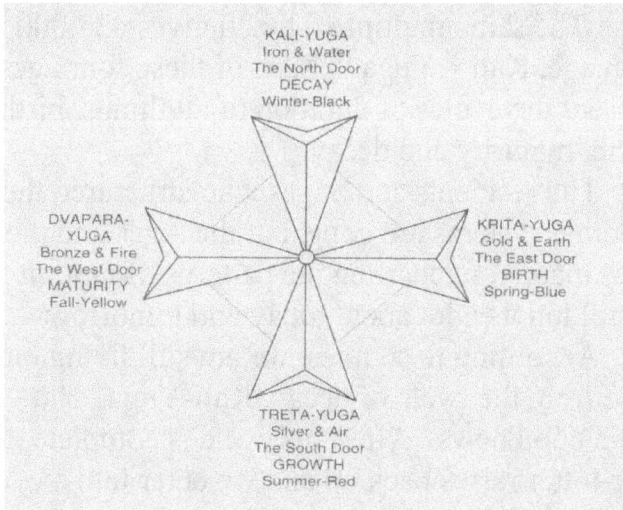

This Golden Age will be ruled by the earth's elements and all live on the earth. Everything, including the earth {*Beloved Babajeran*}, will be reborn at this time. This cycle is also ruled by the priesthood, so I am sure that during Krita - Yuga we can expect to see the rebirth of many useful and beautiful spiritual ceremonies. During Kali -Yuga, even though it is a cycle of decay, many seeds will be planted that will sprout during the age of Gold. *{In the Tarot Krita – Yuga is symbolized by the suite of cups.}*

Source: Freedom Star by Lori Adaile Toye, pages 72 - 74

http://www.iamamerica.com/

INVOCATIONS

*For
Personal
and
Planetary
use*

*For
Healing
and
Transformation*

HEART, HEAD AND HAND DECREES

Heart

Violet Fire, thou love divine,
Blaze within this heart of mine!
Thou art mercy forever true,
Keep me always in tune with you.

Head

I AM light, thou Christ in me,
Set my mind forever free;
Violet fire, forever shine
Deep within this mind of mine.

God who gives my daily bread,
With Violet fire fill my head
Till thy radiance heaven like
Makes my mind a mind of light

Hand

I AM the hand of God in action,
Gaining victory every day;
My pure soul's great satisfaction
Is to walk the Middle Way.

[Repeat 3 times each]

Tube of Light Decree

Beloved I AM Presence Bright,
Round me seal your tube of light
From Ascended Masters flames
Called forth now in God's own name.
Let it keep my temple free
From all discord send to me.

I AM calling forth the Violet Fire
To blaze and transmute all desire,
Keeping on in freedoms name
Till I AM one with the Violet Flame

[Repeat 3 times]

I AM THE LIGHT OF THE HEART

I AM the light of the hearth
Shinning in the darkness of being
And changing all into
The golden treasury
Of the mind of Christ.

I AM projecting my love
Out into the world
To erase all errors
And to break down all barriers.

I AM the power of infinite love,
Amplifying itself
Until it is victorious,
World without end!

[Repeat 3 times]

Let the fiat of the Lord be with me *[9x]*

Mantra

1. O Saint Germain, send Violet Flame;
Sweep it through my very core;
Blessed Zadkiel, Oromasis,
Expand and intensify more and more.
2. O Jesus, send thy Violet Flame,
Sanctify my very core;
Blessed Mary, in God's name,
Expand and intensify more and more.
3. O Mighty I AM, send Violet Flame
Purify my very core;
Maha Chohan, Thou Holy One.
Expand, expand God's lovely sun.

[repeat 9 times after every stanza]:
Right now blaze through and saturate,
Right now expand and penetrate,
Right now set free God's mind to be,
Right now and for eternity.

**I AM a being of Violet Fire
I AM the purity God Desires!**

*[Repeat the last 2 stanzas 49 times visualizing that
you're standing in the center of a
Pillar of Violet Fire]*

In the name of Almighty God
Saint Germain, help me now!

VIOLET FIRE!

Great Cosmic Light,
Come forth and blaze here!
Angelic hosts, come forth and blaze
Thy might light rays through these,
Thy people!
Angels of Saint Germain and El Morya,
Come forth and blaze the Will of God
And the power of transmutation, in the holy name of
freedom, through this place and out into the world of
form, until everyone upon earth feels a great release of
the pressure of that substance known as sin and human
discord from their worlds!
Erase and erase and erase the memory
~ cause effect and power ~
Of these conditions from their beings,
And let them enter the new world
With a clean slate, wiped clean this night
By the power of the Violet Flame!
O Violate Flame, O Violet Flame,
O Violate Flame!
In the name of God, In the name of God,
In the name of God!
O Violate Flame! O Violate Flame!
O Violet Flame!
Flood the world, and flood the world,
And flood the world,
In the I AM name, in the I AM name,
In the I AM name!
Peace and peace and peace,
Be spread throughout the earth!

May the Orient express peace,
May the Occident express peace,
May peace come from the East
And go to the West,
Come from the North and go to the South,
And circle the world around!
May the swaddling garments of the earth
Be in place to magnify the Lord
In this day and hour and this night.
May the world abide in an aura of God-Peace.

And in full faith, I consciously accept this manifest,
manifest, manifest!   [*Repeat 3 times*]
Right here and now with full power, eternally
sustained, all-powerfully active, ever expanding and
world enfolding until all are wholly ascended in the
light and free!

Beloved I AM, Beloved I AM, Beloved I AM!

THE KEEPER'S DAILY PRAYER
By Ascended Master Lady Nada

A flame is active ~
A flame is vital ~
A flame is eternal ~
I AM a God flame of radian love
From the very heart of God
In the Great Central Sun,
Descending from the Master of Life!
I AM charged now
With beloved Helios and Vesta's
Supreme God Consciousness
And solar awareness.
Pilgrim upon earth,
I AM walking daily the way
Of the ascended masters victory
That leads to my eternal freedom
By the power of the sacred fire
This day and always,
Continuously made manifest
In my thoughts, feelings and
Immediate awareness,
Transcending and transmuting
All the elements of earth
Within my four lower bodies
And freeing me by the power of the sacred fire
From those misqualified foci of energy
Within my being.
I AM set free right now from all that binds
By and through the currents
of the divine flame

Of the secret fire itself,
Whose ascending actions makes me
God in manifestation,
God in action,
God in direction, and
God in consciousness!
I AM an active flame!
I AM a vital flame!
I AM an eternal flame!
I AM an expanding fire spark
From the Great Central Sun
Drawing to me now every ray
Of divine energy which I need
And which can never be
Re-qualified by the human
And flooding me with the light
And God-illumination of a thousand suns
To take dominion and rule supreme forever
Everywhere I AM!
Where I AM, there God is also,
Unseparated forever I remain,
Increasing my light
By the smile of his radiance,
The fullness of his love,
The omniscience of his wisdom,
And the power of his life eternal,
Which automatically raises me
On ascension wings of victory
That shall return me to the heart of God
From whence in truth,
I AM come to do God's will
And manifest abundant life to all!

A CALL TO THE FIRE BREATH OF GOD!

I AM, I AM, I AM the fire breath of God
From the heart of beloved Alpha and Omega.
This day I AM the immaculate concept
In expression everywhere I move.

Now I AM full of joy,
For now, I AM the full
Expression of divine love.

My beloved I AM Presence,
Seal me now within the very heart
Of the expanding fire breath of God.
Let its purity, wholeness and love
Manifest everywhere I AM today and forever!

I accept this done right now with full power!
I AM this done right now with full power!
I AM, I AM, I AM God-life expressing
Perfection all ways at all times.

This, which I call forth for myself
I call forth for every man, woman,
And child on this planet.

TRANSFORMATIVE AFFIRMATIONS
Of Jesus the Christ

I AM THAT, I AM
I AM the open door, which no man can shut
I AM the light, which lightens every man that cometh
into the world,
I AM the way, I AM the truth, I AM the life,
I AM the resurrection,
I AM the ascension in the light.
I AM the fulfillment of all my needs and
Requirements of the hour,
I AM abundant supply poured out upon all life.
I AM perfect sight and hearing,
I AM the manifest perfection of being,
I AM the illimitable light of God
Made manifest everywhere,
I AM the light of the holy of holies.
I AM the son of God,
I AM the light of the holy mountain of God

I AM THE VIOLET FLAME

I AM the Violet Flame
In action in me now
I AM the Violet Flame
To light alone I bow
I AM the Violet Flame
In mighty cosmic power
I AM the light of God
Shinning every hour
I AM the Violet Flame
Blazing like a Sun
I AM God's secret power
Freeing everyone.

{Repeat 49 times}

CELLULAR AWAKENING FOR HUMANITY
By Master Jesus/Sananda

Great Light of Divine Wisdom,
Stream forth to my being,
And through your right use
Let me serve mankind and the planet.
Love, from the Heart of God,
Radiate my being with the presence of the Christ
That I walk the path of truth.
Great source of creation,
Empower my being,
My brother,
My sister,
And my planet
With perfection
As we collectively awaken as One Cell.
I call forth the Cellular Awakening.
Let wisdom, love, and power stream forth to this cell,
This cell that we all share.
Great spark of creation awaken the
Divine Plan of Perfection.
So we may share the ONE perfected cell,
I AM.

COMMAND TO THE YELLOW LIGHT
By Ascended Master Saint Germain

In the name of the Christ, my Real Self, and by the power of the Three Fold Flame within my heart, I command that My Great God Self, balance the flow of Love, Wisdom, and Power within my four lower bodies.

So it is, Amen!

COME BLESS US DEAR MOTHER!

Oh Goddess,
Inspirational source of Gods and immortals,
You that are Fertile, Abundant and Free,
Mother of All, who brings forth the bounty
Of fruits and good cheer,
Satisfy our Souls, our Hearts, and our Needs.

Adored Maiden, who flows out in space
While we, your children are not aware,
That if not for your love
And commitment to care
We would be a lost speck,
Out there, somewhere.

Yet by your loving kindness,
You do nature's work
And allow the infinite
To be part of the scheme;
As if by some miracle, we could set free
The magic in heaven, in life, and in thee.

Immortal, Blessed,
Crowned with Every Grace,
Deep bosomed Earth,
It is you, we venerate.

Sweet plains, fragrant fields,
Your grass nourished by the rain,
While the sun grows thy fertile seeds
That will bring us harvest in the early spring.

Give us your blessings today Dear Mother.
Come; bless your children, again and again.
Today and always, love and provide us
With our daily bread from thy earthly grains.

May our bounty be prosperous.
May our needs be less.
May our hearts be full
Of your tender caress.

OUR LADY MARY OF CHARITY
Patron Saint of Cuba

To you we come, O Holy Mother
Honoring the love you've given us.
And ask that you guide us to a better morrow
Without the anxieties that betray our pleas.

We ask that Cuba and all its people
Come together to love and to rebuilt,
A blissful oasis in the land of plenty
Where peace and harmony is all that exist.

May our children grow under your embrace
As all Cubans before them have done.
May we come together from all over the world
To honor your essence,
Your love and your grace.

Blessed are thou Mary of Charity,
Blessed is the heart that soothes our pain.
Everywhere we go your name is revered
As if, the name Mary
Was sketched in our cells.

Your love displays your might and power,
Building the momentum
That will bring true peace,
To this lovely nation and to all its people.
We thirst and we hunger
For the peace you give.

PRAYER TO VENUS
The Evening Star

By John Fletcher,
Elizabethan poet & playwright

O Divine Star of Heaven,
Thou in power above the seven:
Thou sweet kindler of desires
Till they grow to mutual fires:
Thou, O gentle Queen that art
Curer of each wounded heart:
Thou the fuel, and the flame;
Thou in Heaven and here the same:
Thou the wooer, and the woo'd:
Thou the hunger, and the food:
Thou the prayer, and the pray'd:
Thou what is, or shall be said:
Thou still young, and golden tressed,
Make me by thy answer blessed.

HAIL MARY
Nondenominational

Hail, Mary, full of grace
The Lord is with thee.
Blessed art thou among women
And blessed is the fruit of thy womb, Jesus.

Holy Mary, Mother of God
Pray for us, sons, and daughters of God,
Now and at the hour of our victory,
Over sin, disease, and death.

I AM LORD'S PRAYER
Nondenominational

Our Father who art in heaven
Hallowed be thy name, I AM.
I Am thy kingdom come,
I AM thy will being done
I AM on earth even as I AM in heaven.
I AM giving this day bread to all
I AM forgiven all life this day even as
I AM also all life is forgiving me
I AM leading all men away from temptation
I AM delivering all men from
Every evil condition
I AM the kingdom
I AM the power and
I AM the glory of God in eternal –
Immortal manifestation, all this, I AM.

PRAYER FOR SELF-LOVE AND ASCENSION

From the Lord God of my Being,
I AM That, I AM, I decree:
I have Love for my journey into my Ascension.
I have Compassion for all physical and emotional pain
I still need to heal.
I give thanks that I am now healing the past and
resurrecting the new.
As a Master of Divine expression, walking the earth,
I now turn on the Light of my Divinity.
I now activate and transform my DNA to its fifth
dimensional potential.
I now choose to completely heal and rejuvenate my
physical body.
I choose to remain happy, harmonious, and grateful.
I claim the mastery that is mine to manifest
my freedom.
I allow my Divinity to manifest in a most wonderful
way.
I give thanks that it is done according to God's Holy
Will!
I call for shafts of Ascension Light to blaze through
me daily and hourly.
So be it, beloved I AM!

[Repeat 3 times}

Source: The Ascension Flame of Purification and
Immortality by Aurelia Louise Jones - page 47

INVOCATIONS TO THE
GOLDEN PINK RAY

In the name of the victorious Presence of God I AM, I call to the heart of Beloved Separis Bey and the Brotherhood of the Ascension Flame at Luxor. I call Beloved Saint Germain, Beloved Jesus/Sananda, Beloved Sanat Kumara, and Lady Venus. I also call the Seven Mighty Elohim, the Seven Beloved Archangels, and the Seven Chohans of the Seven Rays. I now invoke the Golden Pink Ray from the Heart of God to enfold my four main body systems and all my other subtle bodies and I say:

Golden Pink Light from the Heart of God.   *[3 times]*
Infuse my form with thy dazzling Golden Pink radiance.
Saturate me with the Golden Pink Light from above.
Saturate me with the Pure-White Ascension Flame.
Raise me up into Thy Eternal Glory.
Resurrect my entire consciousness, being, and world.
Illumine and charge me with the Light of Cosmic Love for the Victory of my Ascension and for the Victory of my Eternal Freedom in the Light.
As I call this for myself and for the Earth, I also call this for every man, woman and child on this planet.
So be it, beloved I AM!

[Repeat 3 times]

PREPARING

MIND, HEART, & SOUL

FOR OUR ASCENSION

WHAT IS ASCENSION?

ASCENSION is exactly what the word implies, it means 'going up', as to descent [its' opposite] implies going down.

We think of ASCENSION as belonging only to the saints. We think so little of ourselves that we cannot fathom any mortal receiving such grace. Yet, what mortals neglect to see is that in reality, everyone ASCENDS.

As you learn and grow, you evolve. When you learn something new, a shift occurs in the mind giving way to the density of the body, making it lighter. As you meditate the vibratory rate of your body rises. For it is writing 'a man who meditates is making amends and attuning for his ASCENSION'.

The ASCENSION process is not solely for those privileged few who the catholic religion has canonized. While some of those canonized beings are examples of virtues, this book is not about them. This book however, is for the other 99.9% of humanity whom wanting to do good, feel they have failed and expect very little good to come their way.

Let me put your mind to rest; the one ASCENDING is Planet Earth. This book is not about your perfection or imperfection as much as saying that we, her children need to lighten our body so that our Mother is able to take her new position among the stars and other planets in our galaxy.

Traveling lighter implies learning to activate and effectible use our light bodies in order to help our mother in her ASCENSION.

Everything that you have heard in regards to doom day scenarios and theories of the end of the world, is nothing more than the world as we know it, will cease to exist, allowing the dawning of the New Age of Enlightnment to come forth. The Earth will still be the Earth and we will be her children; hopefully, we will be better behaved, more loving, and best suited for our new lives aboard our shining star.

Let us not forget that as Earths' Children, we are aboard our mother ship and she needs our help in order to reach her new destination. As her children, we need to be diligent and purposeful as to insure a safe passage for ourselves as well as helping others to do likewise.

This book's intention is to activate your spiritual cells. As you read and re-read its text, your spiritual cells will awaken and you will know what you need to do when the time comes.

Word of caution: Do not worry about anything. Worry brings your energies down which is totally the opposite of what you want to accomplish. Instead, use your time and precious energy to make your new life ready, TODAY!

PREPARING THE ASTRAL BODY
FOR ASCENSION

The feeling of floating outside the body is known as, *'an out of body experience'*. An out of body experience is a scientifically proven phenomenon. This experience happens frequently to those who mediate regularly.

An out of body experience is also known as an *'astral projection'*, especially when it is done intentionally. There have been numerous substantiated reports of people who when near death start the process of projecting themselves voluntarily outwardly. There are those who once out of the body go up and look down upon themselves having no emotional consequences in seeing what their physical body is experiencing.

I am grateful that humanity has come to accept *'an out of body experience'* as real. I know that when you hear something repeatedly, eventually we get it. Understanding this important aspect of ourselves is vital. An ***Astral Body Experience*** is one of humanities greatest assets in our collective spiritual awakening.

It is estimated that about one in ten people will have an out of body experience some time during their lifetime. With so many people having this experience and offering supporting data, it has become impossible to dismiss astral travel as a simple imaginary incident.

Now imagine being able to learn how to project yourself outwardly and have your astral body travel at night as you comfortably sleep. You already do, except you are unaware of what is happening.

In spirit, we are *conscious*, our actions are *deliberate,* and our work is *constant.* These are key elements that we need to do in our waking state. This trio is vital to our victory in any undertaking.

Learning to command your Astral Body to go where you want it to go is making sure that it will learn what you need or want to learn. Perhaps you want to go to a specific place; perhaps you want to be with a particular Ascended Master and learn a subject from him or her while your body is sleeping comfortably in bed.

While many claim that astral body is an involuntary event and for all practical reasons, this is a true statement, what I am introducing is being deliberate by stating where you want to go before going to sleep.

Please remember that you are a soul having a physical experience and that you are a powerful and adventurous being. The only thing that is new is learning to trust that which we are. Trust your powers, trust who you are and know that the outcome can only be beneficial to you, your life, and to those around you.

Energy is all that is! Your soul is energy. Even the dense part of the human body is also energy. What makes the body a bulky mass is the perception that it is dense, however when put under scrutiny, the human body is light as air. However, for argument sake let us supposed that we are indeed a bulky mass and that in addition to our physical body, due to our collective ignorance we have created three other bodies, which are as heavy, if not more than as the physical body is.

These bodies are real, and their names are; the mind body, the emotional body, and the pain body.

What makes this fact so interesting is that even though we are not conscious of our thoughts, words, and actions, we most have done something right for now we have the opportunity of fixing pass errors.

If you are reading this book, this implies that something inside of you has changed, you are searching for answers to life and you have finally accepted that you are worthy of having a better existence.

As you start the work that is before you, as you learn to control, and change your thoughts and emotions, you will realize that pain comes from not understating what is taking place in your life. Fix all that brings you pain by shedding light on the situation and soon your bodies will be lighter.

As you star to meditate regularly, as you incorporated in your daily routine the reading of the affirmations and decrees in this book, [as well as others of your choosing] the change I speak of and the change you seek will be inevitable.

Not too long ago, I remember a Rina that did no respect her body. Is a matter of fact I had no self-love. Yet something guided me to find that who was missing from my life was I. Change is not an over night remedy; nothing that is transformative is. However, the work I did and continue doing, prove to be of great value in every aspect of the person I AM today.

I feel such gratitude for who I use to be as much as, for who I have become. If nothing more, when I knew little wanted a better life and my desire of change took me to find answers. Wisdom comes to everyone. It is part of who we are. All we have to do is be open to experience something other than and the experience and the wisdom will appear.

What I give you in this book are the words that inspired and motivated me to find within myself what I was missing. I am not asking you to do anything that I have not already done and know of their goodness in every respect.

Because of the work done, today I respect the person I AM. As I also respect my body, mind, heart, and soul. Of all my blessings feel that the greatest one is having love for the journey itself as well as knowing that life's truth is found in every face, smile and place.

Knowing where you are and starting to learn something new from that place is how life changes. Not accepting change or different views is how life becomes stagnate.

"Today I have joy in my life and know that only good can come my way". Life cannot get any easier than this. Of all the things that I have stated, no other can ever be as powerful or as simple as this is.

I respect my body because I know that is the temple of my soul, the casing, the housing, of what is eternal in me. I also know that my soul has powers and mysteries, which are mine to discover, understand and use correctly for the good of mankind.

I have never been able to accept half-truths. Anything that I have heard that makes no sense, have dismissed from the unset. Perhaps this is the reason why I have not really been confused about my spirituality. Confronted, yes; confused no!

When you know who you are, why you are here, and what you are here to do, very little changes inside of who you are. If anything what happens is that, who you are takes a hold of your senses making confusion impossible. Then my dear friends, is when the true magic begins, and never stops.

What follows is one of many Etheric Temples ~ Retreats that you can travel to in your Astral Body. This particular Temple is located over the Island of Cuba. As you travel in your Astral Body, night after night, you will come to see how clear and simple life becomes. The more you give yourself the freedom, to travel in the Astral Body and visit the various retreats available to you, that is when an Ascended Master will take you under his or her tutelage. Learning cannot get any better than this.

As you practice, you will be preparing the Astral Body for the upcoming transition. Travel far, and travel in the light. And as you do, open your Higher Mind to the Universal Heart so that the true meaning of love can become part of the new person you are becoming. Enjoy the experience of a lifetime and share it with others.

ARCHANGEL ZADKIEL AND HOLY AMETHYST ETHERIC TEMPLE ~RETREAT

Archangel Zadkiel and Holy Amethyst have their Etheric Temple ~ Retreat over the Island of Cuba. They are the Archangels of the Violet Flame of Freedom also known as The Temple of Purification. This retreat was physical before the sinking of Atlantis. Back then, Cuba was known, as the *Amethyst Island* and its land mass was greater in size than in present day. Here, students come in their Astral Bodies to receive the alchemical training from ancient priests and priestesses under the Order of Melchizedek.

The Temple of Purification releases the Violet Flame of Freedom, Forgiveness, and Transmutation to the Planet, from its Central Temple and other Six Minor Temples. The Central Temple is a round edifice with a golden dome where the Violet Flame of Freedom blazes, midst Amethyst Crystals. Archangel Zadkiel and Holy Amethyst invite students to come to the Temple to learn the true meaning of Spiritual Freedom.

Call to attend the Temple: In the name of the Christ, my Own Real Self, I call to the Heart of my Mighty I AM Presence, to the Angel of the Presence, to Beloved Archangel Michael, Kuan Yin, and the Maha Chohan. Take me to the Temple of Purification over the Island of Cuba, according to the will of my Holy Christ Self and the direction of the Maha Chohan. I ask to receive instruction on the law of freedom and the formula for the victory of the flame of freedom within my heart and seat-of-the-soul chakra, especially as it pertains to the gifts of prophecy.

(personal prayer)

<u>Gratitude:</u> Beloved Archangel Zadkiel and Holy Amethyst, help me to remember upon awakening all that will help me to fulfill my mission on earth and the mission of my twin flame. I accept this call manifested through the power of my individualize Christ and I am thankful for its realization. In the name of the Father, the Son, the Holy Spirit and the Divine Mother, Amen!

Now a day Ancon Beach, Sancti Spiritus, Villa Clara, Cuba

"Energy follows thought. Your voice has power and your word is a command to action. Action is the verb; your word is the fuel that will ignite the flame of your soul. Let the magic begin".

REVEALING THE SECRET POWERS OF SUNRISE AND TWILIGHT

Who is not moved by the beautiful display of love at Sunrise and Twilight? No matter who you are, we all find a reason to look up at the sky at this time of day. We love to gaze at this magnificent sight as if we knew the secrets it holds not yet revealed to modern man. What is amazing is that once we discover these secrets and learn to align mind, heart, and soul to Nature's Wisdom, many treasures are unveiled. From them on, you will not stop wanting to learn every secret Father Sky and Mother Earth hold.

In this lesson, we will be addressing one of many Nature's well-kept secrets. All I ask is that you use it well, consciously and often, and soon you will see the difference that doing something so small, yet powerful can do for you.

Let us begin. The secret behind Sunrise and Twilight is found in its colors. For the most part, the colors in the sky at this time of day are Blue and Pink. The combination of these two colors is Violet. What makes this combination so powerful is not the Violet color itself, but its greater mystery is that inside the Violet hue there is a Golden Substance or Energy. This Golden Substance found in the Violet hue, is also present in one of our aura, # 6th outer layer, as well as in Planet Earth's 6th outer layer or aura.

This layering of colors and its transformation from one to another is called Alchemy. These alchemical transfers have the power to change a substance into other than. As we become more in tune with our spiritual powers, we will learn how to change aspects of our personality by using alchemy.

The Golden Substance found in the Violet Hue in ancient times was used by wise sages to fortify their auras as well as other alchemical treatments. An alchemist transforms or transmutes any condition, situation, or karma by purifying the tendency, habit, or inclination to one of a higher vibration.

While the Golden Substance or Energy found at Sunrise and Twilight can be used for various treatments, we will use it to awaken the Eight-Sided Cell of Perfection that is in our hearts and to strengthen our 6th outer layer or aura, known as our Evolutionary Body.

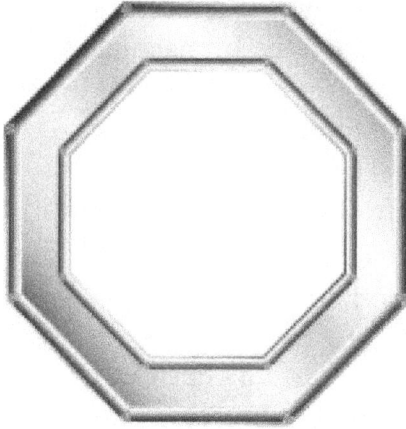

AWAKENING THE EIGHT- SIDED CELL OF PERFECTION

Among the many spiritual attributes that our heart has, The Eight-Sided Cell of Perfection is perhaps one of the most important ones. While the topic of this lesson is the eight-sided cell of perfection, thought that it would be of interest to my readers, if the other spiritual attributes found in the hear were also mentioned.

In the physical body, the heart is the most important muscle. With every beat, it sends us the signal that life is running through us. Yet seldom does anyone pay attention to the heart's mechanism, its functions, or that with every beat it gives life.

Perhaps, humans are too busy to pay attention to the one that keeps us doing what we love to do, which is to live our life. Or maybe the reason why we are ungrateful is that we are unaware that in spirit, the heart holds many treasures.

Beside the eight-sided cell of perfection, in our hearts, we also have the Immaculate Concept, represented by a trio of colors, also known as 'The Christ Within', those colors are:

- Sapphire Blue, God's Divine Will,
- Golden Yellow, God's Divine Intelligence,
- Pink, God's Divine Love.

In the center of this beautiful trio is the White Flame of the Christ, represented by The Divine Mother or Female Principal and the Unfed Flame, the Monad or Masculine Principal, in its center is the eight-sided cell of perfection.

Why is this cell so important? Activating this cell equals activating your spiritual perfection. In time and as you continue working on its growth you will reach **"Unana, the Consciousness of ONENESS"**. You will continue growing until you stop being a HUMAN to become a **'UMAN, The Universal Man'**.

Among the many fallacies, that humanity has created, there is the one of engaging in repeating an untruth, creating a myth. One of these myths is the term Anti Christ. As expected, the term or word is associated to something of demonic nature. Sorry to spoil your appetitive for the gruesome or the need to create unnecessary fear for yourself and other, but nothing can be further from the truth. The Anti Christ is the un-manifested Christ within you. When the Christ in you awakens, your imperfections will be made perfect. As you turn on the Light of Your Divinity, you will become "The Hallowed One".

This is how important you are. This is how precious you are. This is how much you are loved. Guidance, assistance and help, are but seconds away. *"So I say onto you, ask, and it will be given onto you; seek, and you will find; knock, and it will be opened onto you" Luke.* These are not empty promises. These words embody the true essence of your spiritual heritage! When you can realize the importance of your role in life, then will you be able to understand that no moment has ever been better than the present, and that no time has ever been more appropriate, than the here and now. For eons, we have been coming to Planet Terra getting ready for the upcoming events. As we united, as we come to the realization of our greatness, as we learn to accept and embrace our powerful truth, we will meet our fate in love, and in full glory, we will be victorious. That is our destiny!

Meditation: Using the Golden Light or Energy found at Sunrise and Twilight we will begin our meditation. *First* call your I AM Presence, and your Holy Christ Self; call the Ascended Master that you are working with and after having placed the call say the following words:

"OMANEA PATEA HAITAKA"

This call is an acknowledgement to the I Am Presence within the Violet Flame and a call Ascended Master Saint Germain. The meaning of the phrase is,

I Am the see-er of the Lord. So be it!

Please note: to do this work you will need a good imagination *{Imagination is the Greatest Nation in the World}*, also *nostrils, Third Eye Chakra, {the spot between the eyes} lungs, and heart. *While you will use your nostrils to bring in the energy into your body, you will visualize or imagine that the Golden Light comes into the body through your Third Eye.

1. Slowly breathe in the Golden Light through the Third Eye. Allow the Golden Light to go to the lungs and from the lungs allow the energy to flow into the heart.
2. See how the Gold Light expands inside your heart as it travels through all the hearts chambers awakening all the spiritual secrets that it holds.
3. Envision The Eight-Sided Cell of Perfection awakening and expanding, growing more and more with each breathe you take.
4. Visualize the Third Eye opening as the Golden energy enters the heart and floods the entire body.
5. Visualize your body become gold inside and out. Stay a few minutes making the gold energy vibrant, alive; feel its warmth.
6. Now find the 6th outer layer or aura of your body; look for the colors of Violet and Gold that are inside the 6th outer aura. Tap into its colors and see the colors expand becoming strong, wide, and alive.
7. Notice the purity of the energy in your body.
8. Feel how the beat of your heart slows down.

9. Feel the energy of peace come over mind, body, and soul. Breathe the peace you have become. Now send this peace to all life on Planet Earth

   Make sure that you maintain the same flow of air in every breath; the air you inhale should equal the air that you exhale. If you become lightheaded or your breathing becomes impaired, stop the meditation. Observe your emotional body for possible hidden fears. Fear creates blockages, or energetic obstructions. Once removed continue with the meditation.

   This meditation is to be done during the hours of Sunrise and Twilight. Each meditation should last no more than 20 minutes. The more you practice this meditation the more that you will become perfect.

THE IMPORTANCE
OF A VEGETARIAN DIET

"Nothing can be more beneficial to human health while increasing the chances of survival of life on Earth, than the change to a vegetarian diet."

~ Albert Einstein

The basis of morality is the recognition within man that gives way to understanding that he is an intrinsic part of Nature and that he is inter-connected to life as to the great cosmic ensemble. This is the fundamental notion needed to understand the importance of life itself. Once man comes to this conclusion, he will assist all life form on the planet with his compassion.

If there is an aspect of humanity, where The Law of Unity is of vital importance, it is in Nutrition. Even if you consider meat to be a good choice, there are many who differ from your assessment. In India, about 70% of the population eats a vegetarian diet. Those that do, live longer and healthier lives than those who eat meat.

In today's' supermarket, you see the meat already pre-packaged and because of this, its true origin escapes us. What we do not see through the cellophane is that inside the meats we eat, is nothing more than dead flesh from an animal that was killed for our consumption.

Wait there is more. When the animal is killed, its' fear turns into poison. This poison travels the entire body of the animal and goes into every cell. This is what those who eat meat really eat. In reality, you are eating fear. Fear of a dead animal can only give you fear and decay. There is no nutritional value found in fear.

This book is not about cruelty to animals. Our actions should be evidence that indeed we are cruel and inhumane. However, this lesson is to make you aware of what you are doing to yourself when you ingest the flesh of a dead animal. *Nothing that has a face, nothing that has eyes should be eating by humans.*

The only reason why some of us still eat flesh is because the animal cells inside of us are still alive and they dictate the need to eat what ones sustained and nourished us. While today, the need to eat meat does not exist, the memory of having done so is still alive inside the cells. The aspect of the psyche that needs healing is the side who believes that it has to do what it used to do when it was an animal. Since we no longer roam or hunt to survive, the need to eat meat is false.

As the individual gets older, the digestion slows down making eating meats impossible in some cases. Why do you think this happens? If meat was good for our health and if meat had nutritional value, don't you think that the human body would have adjusted its digestive system so that men could eat meat? Why do you suppose it has not? In reality, it does the opposite, does it not? Could it be that the intolerance of our digestion is a reflection of what we eat?

The commercials on TV, in their majority, are for digestive problems. Why do you suppose that is? These commercials are incentives so that you keep on eating what you should not eat. Is as saying; go ahead, eat your life away. However, before you die, buy the product I am selling.

Want the cure to your ailment? **"DO NOT EAT ANY MORE MEAT AND YOU WILL ADD 10 TO 15 YEARS TO YOUR LIFE".** Another thing that I want to make my readers aware of is that we should not drink milk either; milk is for calves. No human should drink milk, yet milk is what our children drink, and when they get sick, we do not understand why, after all a doctor told you to give your child milk.

Our responsibility as adults is to use our wits. Too many of us trusts the pharmaceutical companies, doctors, and practitioners and follow someone else's recommendations to later see that their recommendation went against our very nature.

Could it be that you, as an individual should find what is best for you? I am sure that if we got **SMART,** eventually we would stop listening to the lies told by those in control of what sells in the supermarket, what is advertized on TV, the doctors who have a license to practice on you, and by the pharmaceutical, makers of the drugs sold by prescription only.

Here are some reasons why **No Human** should eat meat and why a change to a Vegetarian Diet is recommended:

- Vegetables are is in harmony with the laws of the universe.
- A well-balanced vegetarian diet prevents illness.
- Its absence from our diet will end the creation of karma.
- Controlling the 4 lower bodies becomes easy as the impulses of creating negative tendencies ceases.
- It improves the state of the subtle bodies, (etheric, spiritual, astral body, and others).
- Among the benefits found in a vegetarian diet there are; the purification and transmutation of vices into virtues, and the curative elements found in the solar energy only found in vegetables, fruits and grains.
- You will have more energy as you stop eating unnecessary food.
- As the need to eat heavy foods ceases, you will become more harmonious.
- A well-balanced vegetarian diet prevents heart disease, tumors, and cancers.
- It allows the progressive elimination of toxins caused by the accumulation of gases and others.

- A vegetarian diet gives fulfillment, peace, joy, and an all around wellness.
- The person becomes healthier, stronger and this leads to having good discernment.
- A vegetarian diet brings about unity with nature, you nature and the nature in all that has life.

For these and other reasons, we should take a better look at what we eat and learn to make better choices. Adopt a healthier life style. As souls, we are always evolving, growing, and ascending. When we eat meat, it does not matter how much we meditate, or how many affirmations we repeat. In reality, we are contributing to the opposite of evolution, and as a result, we are condemning all life to perpetual slavery to old and decaying customs, ideas, notions, and habits.

The time is now to prepare the way for a New Life. Changing your nutritional habits is one of the most important things you will ever do, for yourself and for humanity as a whole. Visit your freezer, refrigerator, and pantry, see what is in it, and change what you buy.

I am certain that in the very near future many will become vegetarians, making this new concept popular. You see, a vegetarian diet is in harmony with the laws of the living universe and as such, our souls resonate higher as our connection becomes stronger and brighter, than ever before. Become free; stop eating what can only hurt you!

GRACE

Heavenly Father,
Receive this food. Make it Holy.
Let not the impurity of greed defile it.
This food is from Thee, it is for Thy Temple.
Spiritualize it. Spirit to Spirit goes.
We are the petals of Thy Manifestation.
But Thou are the Flower, Its Life, Beauty,
and Loveliness,
Permeate our souls with the fragrance of
Thy Presence.

Paramhansa Yogananda

Saying this prayer before every meal, will insure a save transition to a vegetarian diet!

PREPARING THE EVOLUTIONARY BODY

All humans have various layers or auras also known as light bodies encompassing our physical body, which protect us at all times. That we do not know this, equals our ill attempt to find how precious and loved we truly are.

I hope that you have been working diligently on the awakening of The Eight-Sided Cell of Perfection for several weeks if not months by now. Moreover, that you have began in earnest a vegetarian diet and have been on it for more than 21 to 24 days.

Now that we have established the perimeters to learning the next lesson, let us proceed.

In previous lessons, we have addressed what you need to do in preparation for working with your light bodies. While throughout this book I have made you privy to vital information, since you have already heard some of your profound spiritual heritage, allow me to tell you more.

As a divine and powerful creature, you have the wherewith all to transform any present state to one that is more in tune to the person you are becoming making sure that you are in alignment to your divine heritage.

If at present you do not feel divine, it behooves you to find out how to activate your spiritual cells so that your present state, condition, situation, or circumstance becomes a more pleasant, rewarding and joyful representation of whom you truly are.

Your only concern while on Planet Earth should be awakening your spiritual powers. However, I am familiar with how the human mind works coupled with a hectic day [created by the mind] leaving very little time to do what should be, your only concern.

Man toils every day to have a roof over his head, food on the table, clothes on his backs, a car on the driveway and money for a rainy day. Except in today's economy, what we call needs have become a burden to upkeep. No material object has ever been ours and learning to let go of what does not belong to us should not be difficult. Yet, keeping what is not ours has become our main focus.

As man struggles to become other than what he truly is, he has managed to confuse his life by desiring to have material possessions. ___No thing___ that burns, brakes, or gets lost, comes from spirit. It is not blessed, and it does not have the power to satisfy you.

Man, in his confused state of mind has become greedy and selfish leaving little room for spirit to be front and center in his every day life. However, life as we know it, will soon come to an end. Reason why man's need to make amends with himself and with life has never been greater nor has his need to find the depth of his soul ever had so much meaning.

As stayed at the opening of this lesson, all human beings have several layers of protection, one of which is the Evolutionary Body, our 6th aura. The word 'evolution' means, to evolve, to grow, to develop, to progress, to advance. You will notice that as you learn to use the Evolutionary Body, it will be easy to move in and out, to and from other dimensions.

If you have completed the work in the previous lessons then by now you are familiar with finding the 6th outer aura. Using the same technique, in your mind's eye go to the Evolutionary Body and concentrate on its colors of Violet and Gold for 5 minutes in the first meditation, 10 minutes the second meditation, until you have reached 20 minutes. Look for the colors of Violate and Gold in the Evolutionary Body and see yourself become *ONE* with the colors and with the aura itself. See the colors become brilliantly bright. Make them so bright that they mesmerize you.

When you place your attention on 'something', that which you are putting your attention on expands, grows, it even becomes tridimensional. Your job is to use your spiritual sight to make this Light Body stronger. This is what is known as turning what is dense into light, luminous, airy energy.

I cannot emphasis enough the need to meditate, meditate, and meditate again. Be patient with the process as with yourself knowing that, soon the light within you will be ready for you to assist the Planet in her Ascension.

Keep doing the work and know that the day will come when it will be your turn to teach others. When you know you teach. When you have, you give. Nothing that you have learned or owned is yours. A generous heart is full of love and this is the only thing that truly matters. As your heart shines, you become connected to all life in our universe and this makes you magical and immortal!

CONNECTING THE HUMAN EVOLUTIONARY BODY TO EARTHS'

As humans, Planet Earth also has a 6th outer layer, also known as the Evolutionary Body. Our job is to connect the two. This insures safe passage aboard our Mother Ship as she travels to her new position in our galaxy.

If we took the time to see who and what we are, doing this is nothing out of the ordinary. All we would need to accomplish the task is to have the willingness to adapt to the new concept or idea that is being offered us.

Please remember to call your I Am Presence and Christ Self before beginning or doing any meditation, decree, or affirmation. When ready answer the following questions honestly.

1. Have you ever walked barefooted on grass?
2. Have you ever asked Mother Earth to bless you with her *good energy*?
3. Have you ever seen Mother Earth's energy?
4. Have you noticed that her energy looks like Gold Dust?
5. Have you felt her energy entering through your feet?
6. Have you ever felt how the energy goes to your ankles?
7. How about to your legs?
8. What about your knees?
9. How does it feel when it moves throughout your body?

10. Have you ever seen your feet become roots?
11. Have you ever planted your feet in the ground?
12. How big can you make your roots [feet] become?
13. Have you ever seen your roots become so big that they touch the Earth's center?
14. Have you asked Mother Earth to bless you while there?
15. Have you ever blessed her back in gratitude for all she does for you?
16. Have you felt how the tension in your body washes away as you become one with Mother Earth's energy?

If you have not experienced this, I urge you to do so right now. Those who have done it, know its benefits; do it now and then move to the following meditation.

Seated in a comfortable position, visualize your Evolutionary Body perfectly alignment to Mother Earths', making both bodies strong, vibrant, and alive.

Do not merge your energies into hers'; unite both light bodies at feet level. You are on top; she is at your feet. {*See picture*}.

The Evolutionary Body will activate at the command of your voice. This process gives tranquility and wholeness. The more you practice the stronger that both light bodies will become.

Practice doing this at least 3 times a week for 20 minutes each time.

HUMANITY'S STRUGGLES

We can no longer claim that what is outside of us does not affect us, nor can we say that our confused state of mind does not alter our inner peace. Man is in a constant state of flux brought about by his inability to be aware of his true nature.

If you are unconscious, then your senses are under attack and every thing you perceive through them are also in a constant state of flux, the information obtained through your senses cannot be trusted. While using our senses has become second nature, what we neglect to understand is that our senses are tools used to learn, discern, and communicate. In other words, our senses are spiritual gifts.

In today's world, the evidence of what I have stated is too vast and to real to be dismissed by calling it a mere coincidence. That which coincides perfectly is a mathematic equation, which states, 'any occurrence or current, that coincides or collides perfectly with one another, does so by law of attraction'.

Observe your life and see what you are attracting to yourself. Be honest and tell yourself what your life is full of, and start changing your habits to ones that are best suited for the person you are today.

At this moment, after knowing that you are a great light and that you are worthy of having the best life possible, you owe it to yourself to do what ever you have to do to insure that the life you deserve is the life you live.

We are all **ONE** and as such, each one of us has to find their truth within their own heart and come to terms with the fact that in life, in spirit, in nature as in science everything is taking us down **ONE PATH;** *'The Path of Enlightenment'*.

When you become upset, moody, or sad, check your lower bodies; mental, feeling, and pain body, and there you will find what in your absence has changed your outlook on life. If you are not present in your life, *'something else'* will occupy your space.

When an argument erupts, one where you are a bystander, this is the time for you to keep quiet, not the time to add fuel to the fire. Never give an opinion on something that is clearly none of your business, especially when what you say can bring worse consequences.

Collectible, as a Global Society, the need to be responsible in our lives has never been greater. We need to recognize that ignoring our responsibilities is the same as thinking that we can continue doing the same things that has brought us despair and decay.

We are not only responsible to ourselves and to our planet, but we are also responsible to the welfare of our fellowman. Therefore, making sure that we resonate to the heights frequency possible should be our major concern. Becoming aware of our spiritual heritage is how positive change will become real.

I am not asking only **you** to change, that would be preposterous. What I am asking is **FOR all OF US TO CHANGE**. If not **now,** when, and if not **YOU,** who?

Here are some of what needs our immediate attention and consideration:

- Our actions
- Our conduct
- Our lack of conviction
- Our lack of commitment

Work on each one of the above separately and do not stop working on each one, until you can see a new man or woman in the mirror looking back at you. Once you have completed the task, smile, and pad yourself on the back for a job well done.

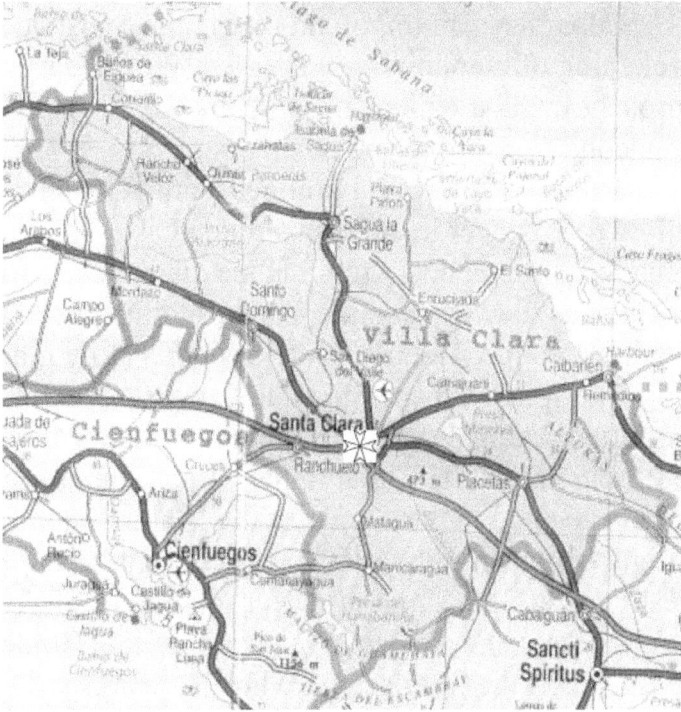

CUBA'S GOLDEN CITY
ITS' VORTEX AND STARS

Province of Villa Clara, Cuba

<u>Its Vortex –Center of the Star is over Santa Clara</u>

<u>Its Radius</u> encompasses the following cities:

<u>South:</u> Manicaragua & Mataguá

<u>West:</u> Santo Domingo & Ranchuelo

<u>North:</u> Sagua la Grande & San Diego del Valle

<u>East:</u> Caibarien & Placetas

Cuba plays an important role in the Spiritual Awakening of humanity. As the New World Order approaches, Cuba will again serve the world by giving her unconditional love and compassion.

The Ray of Divine Intelligence, the Golden Yellow Ray is over its blessed Golden City. Archangel Jophiel and Archill Hope give of their Light and Love as they awaken the Christ Intelligence in the Island, its people, and in all who visit this Holy Place.

The spiritual name given to Cuba's Golden City in spiritual realms is "Asonea". Its Apex is located in the Province of Villa Clara, in the City of Santa Clara, which is located in the Center of the Island. Each Ray of Light comes into its Apex having originated at the Great Central Sun, The Very Heart of God.

The Ascended Master in charge of this Golden City is, Peter, the Everlasting, who also works with the Yellow Golden Ray and both he and the Golden City provide Alignment and Regeneration.

The Spiritual Sound of Asonea is **OM** producing peace and harmony when repeated in a mantra prayer consisting of 108 repetition of the **OM** sound {108 = 9 = 9 is God's Secret Number}.

Every person going to any Golden City, its Vortex, and Star should observe the following protocol:

1. **Make sure** that you have a Diligent Heart and that once started you will continue to do the work in earnest.
2. **Make Sure** that your energy resonates to the Master Teacher that you will be working with.

3. If you do not resonate to a particular teacher, then call upon the Master Teacher that resonates to your energies.
4. **Make sure** that you have been on a Vegetarian Diet for at least 21 to 24 days prior to going into the any Golden City, its Vortex, or Star.
5. Tell your guide how many days, weeks, or months you have been working on the Development of your Evolutionary Body and meditating.

When you meet all the requirements, please follow these steps. **Foot Note:** Stay in each point from 7 to 12 days; DO NOT EXCEED 12 DAYS.

Each Star has eight [8] Adjutant Points and one [1] Center. Each adjutant point has an *Outer and an Inner* most point.

1. 2 Adjutant Points in the South Position.
The *outer* most point is Manicaragua
The *inner* most point is Mataguá
2. 2 Adjutant Points in the West Position
The *outer* most point is Santo Domingo
The *inner* most points is Ranchuelo
3. 2 Adjutant Points in the North Position
The *outer* most point is Sagua la Grande
The *inner* most point is San Diego del Valle
4. 2 Adjutant Points in the East Position
The *outer* most point is Caibarien
The *inner* most point is Placetas

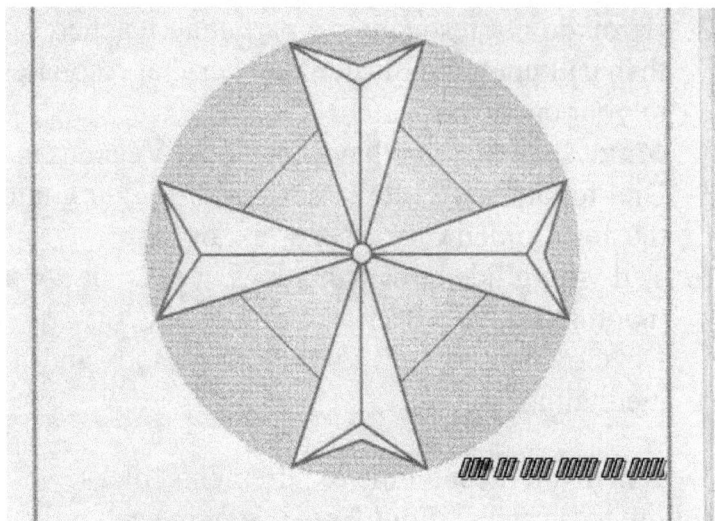

1 center point, the City of Santa Clara = 9 {Nine} Adjutant Points

When approaching any of the 8 Adjutant Points or the Center of the Star, the Heart should be full of love and compassion for all life on Planet Earth, before entering say the following two decrees:

Mightily I AM Presence, Come forth in Thy Luminous Light and Life.
Mightily I AM Presence, I call for Thy Ascension Light and Life.

Now proceed:

1. Go to the ***outer most point*** of the ***South Position***. Stay at this Point for 7 to 12 days. *Note:* this process should not exceed 12 days. When you feel that you are finished

harmonizing your energies with the point, proceed to the next Point.

2. When ready, move to the **_outer_ _most_ _point_** of the **_West Position._** Repeat the phrases and observe the days that you stay at this point not to exceed 12 days.
3. When ready, move to the **_outer_ _most_ _point,_** of the **_North Position._** Repeat the phrases above and familiarize yourself with the energy.
4. When ready, move towards the **_outer_ _most_ _point_** of the **_East Position_** remembering to repeat the phrases and become acquainted with its energy.
5. Once finished with the 4 **_outer_ _most_ _points_** you are ready to **_enter its Center, the Star of Glory._** Repeat the 2 phrases above and familiarize yourself to this mystic energy found here. Please remember that you are entering Hollow Ground. Be aware that as you are receiving its blessings you are also readying your light bodies for Ascension.
6. One you have finished doing the work with the *outer most points,* then process with the **_inner_ _most_ _point_** of each position. When finished, [following the steps already given] enter its center, **_the Star of Glory_** for the second time.

Familiarize yourself with the energy found in each adjutant point *{outer and inner most points}* as well as it center. Move in peace and grace throughout the entire process. For as you do, you will keep the integrity of the energy of this Holy Place ready to give of its blessings to those that follow.

City of Santa Clara, Cuba

CALL TO THE ILLUMINATION FLAME

Illumination Flame from the Heart of God
Expand thy Light through me always.
Golden Flame from the Heart of God
Fill my heart with thy Wisdom Ray.
Illumination Flame from the Heart of God
Expand God's Mind through all my thoughts.
Golden Flame from the Heart of God
Illumine the Earth with thy Golden Light.
Golden Flame from the Heart of God
To thy Love and Light I bow!

[Repeat 3 times]

Topes de Collantes, Sancti Spiritus, Villa Clara, Cuba

Under the Cuban Sky

Spiritual Journeys to Cuba

SEMINAR, WORKSHOPS AND CLASSES

- Awakening the Goddess Within
- The 12 Universal Laws
- Reclaiming your Sexuality
- The Contract of the Soul Seminar

Books Published and soon to be released:

The Contract of the Soul   2008
An Everlasting Love ~ My Father's Poetry 2010
The Contract of the Soul, *Revised Edition* 2011
CUBA: Resurrecting the Amethyst Isle   2011

"I AM DIVINE"

In the quiet moments of the morning
When I rise and greed the day anew,
I contemplate my life in solemn prayer
And give thanks for all, the old and new.

Into the heart, the road that holds all memories,
That holds the imprints of moments long ago,
I see myself as dew from meadows.
Pristine at last I am to love and mold.

And so this morning, as I gaze at life unfolding,
I thank God for each moment that I've lived,
For now, I know that in this perfect moment,
I am Divine my Lord, and always will.

www.ingramcontent.com/pod-product-compliance
Lightning Source LLC
LaVergne TN
LVHW051701080426
835511LV00017B/2660